Helper Robots

Nancy Furstinger

Lerner Publications Company
Minneapolis

Lerner Publications Company
A division of Lerner Publishing Group, Inc.
241 First Avenue North
Minneapolis, MN 55401 USA

For reading levels and more information, look up this title at www.lernerbooks.com.

Cover photo: This robot helps the military disable bombs before they blow up.

Library of Congress Cataloging-in-Publication Data

Furstinger, Nancy, author.
    Helper robots / by Nancy Furstinger.
       pages   cm — (Lightning Bolt Books™ — Robots Everywhere!)
    Summary: What kinds of robots can help humans to deal with disasters? Helper robots!
    Includes index.
    ISBN 978-1-4677-4053-1 (lib. bdg. : alk. paper)
    ISBN 978-1-4677-4690-8 (eBook)
    1. Robots—Juvenile literature. 2. Robotics—Juvenile literature. I. Title.
TJ211.2.F87 2015
629.8'92—dc23   2013045934

Manufactured in the United States of America
1 — BP — 7/15/14

Table of Contents

What is a Robot?

Robots are machines that do work. They move around. They carry out commands.

Some robots look like people.

WABIAN-2

NEDO

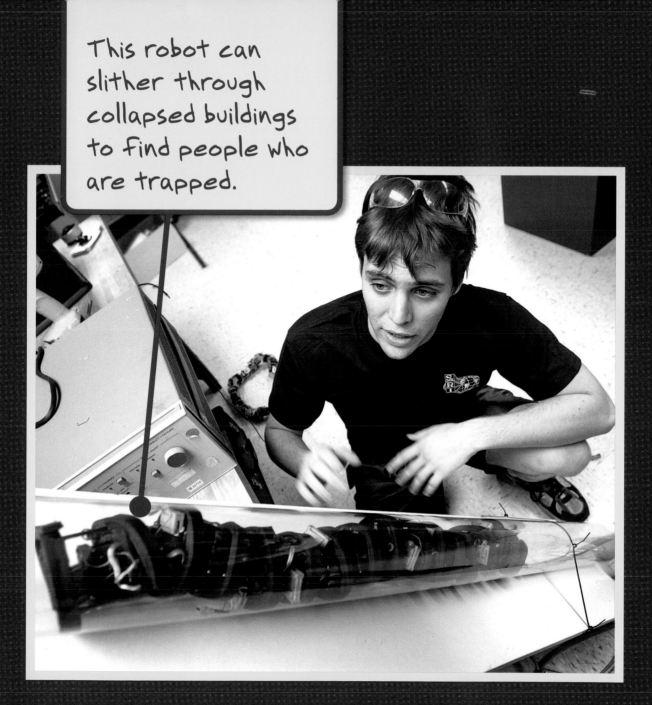

This robot can slither through collapsed buildings to find people who are trapped.

Helper robots come in many shapes and sizes. They do all kinds of jobs. They can work in unsafe places.

Scientists think about hard jobs. They study how robots could help. Then scientists design robots to do that work.

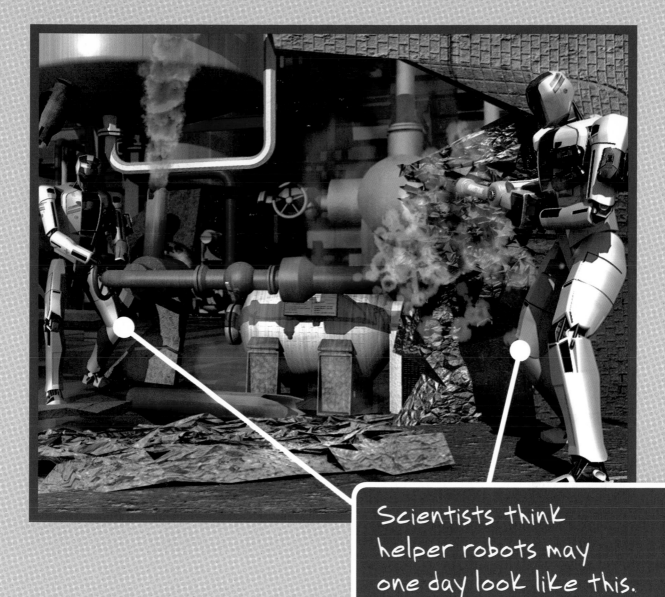

Scientists think helper robots may one day look like this.

Helper robots must be tough. The robots are made of strong metals and plastics.

Helper robots have sensors.
Cameras act as eyes.
Microphones pick up sounds.
Helper robots use lasers to
map the area.

This robot uses
a camera to
get around in
dangerous areas.

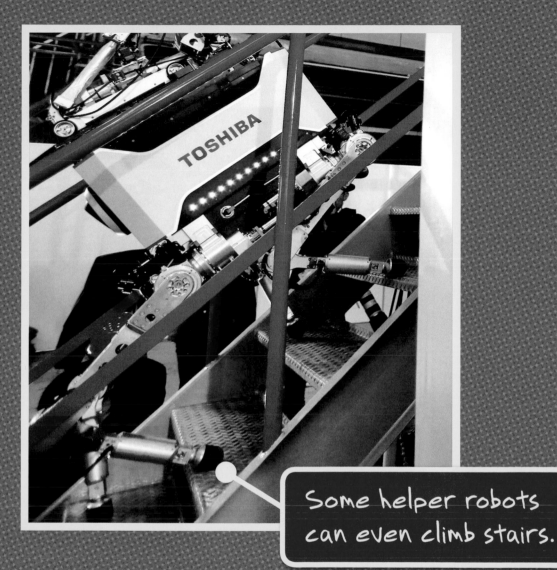

Some helper robots can even climb stairs.

Helper robots move a lot. Some fly over disaster areas. Others use wheels. They drive up and down mountains. Underwater robots move using propellers.

Robots to the Rescue!

Some helper robots work in disasters. They take risks people cannot. Sometimes robots break. New ones can take their place.

This robot is designed to search through collapsed buildings after earthquakes.

Some robots are big enough to carry survivors away from disasters.

The robots explore damage from floods and earthquakes. They crawl through buildings. They look for survivors.

Helper robots are built to handle danger. They have strong motors. Robots use sensors to find trapped people.

Scientists in Japan built a robot named Souryu. It searches for people after disasters.

Scientists practice with rescue robots in special test areas.

Rescue teams guide robots.
Cameras spot trapped people.
Microphones hear yells for help.
Then teams can save people.

The US Navy is building robots to help fight fires on ships.

Some helper robots fight fires. They push rubble away. They carry hoses. Then they spray water on the fire.

Other robots fly over fires.
They take photos. They show
firefighters where to go.

This robot can
hover in place and
take photos.

Dangerous Science

Scientists use helper robots too. These robots teach us about the world. They explore unsafe places. Heat and cold do not stop robots.

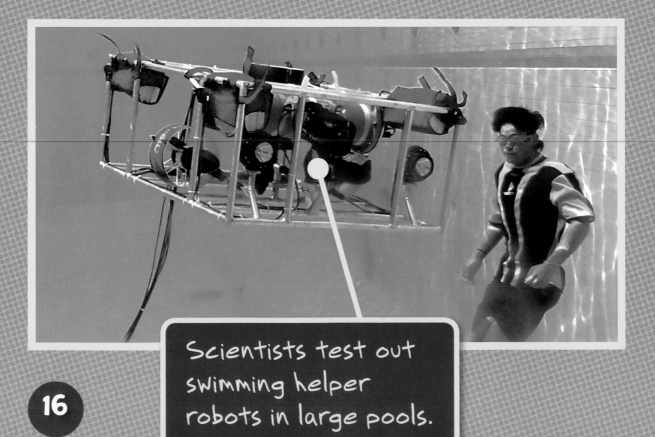

Scientists test out swimming helper robots in large pools.

Robots dive in deep seas. No light reaches these areas. Robots map the seafloor. They even work under thick Arctic ice.

This robot swims under water like an eel.

Some helper robots search for sunken ships. The robots take videos of ships they find. They move in close. They help us learn why the ships sank.

Dr. Robert Ballard shows off Jason Sr., a robot he designed to help find sunken ships.

This robot is named the Ferret. It can be lowered into narrow mine shafts.

Robots also work below the ground. They crawl through caves and mines. Robots help us learn about underground places.

This robot measures earthquakes and poison gases near volcanoes.

Scientists cannot get close to volcanoes. These mountains are filled with hot lava. But robots can.

The robots move across rivers of lava. They travel into hot craters. They pick up melted rock. Sensors measure poison gases.

This photo from a news story shows a helicopter dropping off a robot in a volcano.

Helping the Environment

Some robots help the environment. They collect data about environmental problems. Then scientists study the data.

Science students study data collected by robots.

Flying robots soar through bad weather.

They measure wind. They use cameras to make maps. They help scientists predict storms.

Some robots ski across ice sheets. They study Earth's coldest climates. They drill down into the ground. The robots see how thick snow and ice are. They study how our climate is changing.

The tip of this robot heats up to let it melt through ice sheets.

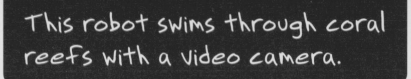
This robot swims through coral reefs with a video camera.

Some helper robots swim in oceans. They explore water currents. This helps us learn how tsunamis start. The robots also learn about coral reefs.

A few ocean robots look like
sea animals. Fish-shaped
robots check water for
pollution. They guide real fish
away from oil spills.

Helper robots have many uses. Scientists keep dreaming up new jobs for them. These amazing robots help keep people safe. They protect the environment too.

If you are in a fire or an earthquake in the future, your rescuer may be a robot.

Robot Scientists

- Robot scientists enjoy math and science. They study engineering and computer programming in school. Many also learn art and design. This helps them come up with creative ideas for robots.

- Robot scientists work in all kinds of places. They might work in labs or classrooms. Some work at disaster sites or aboard ships. They may even work in the Arctic or near volcanoes.

- Kids who want to become robot scientists can study robots in a special program. It is called the **Robotics Academy**. There kids learn how to build robots. Then they compete in contests.

Fun Facts

- Scientists test robots at fake disaster sites. These include fallen buildings and train wrecks.

- One type of robot runs like a cat. It is used for search and rescue. The robot uses springs and small motors to move quickly.

- Another robot twists like a snake. It fits into tight spots. The snake robot can search for people. It looks in caved-in buildings after earthquakes.

- Some new robots can act as an ambulance crew. They will be able to carry medicines, food, and water to trapped people.

- College students in Italy built a new type of robot. It explores volcanoes. It can keep moving even if it gets damaged. Each of its six wheels has its own motor.

Glossary

climate: the average weather in a region

crater: a bowl-shaped hole around the opening of a volcano

disaster: a great misfortune that sometimes happens suddenly

laser: a thin beam of light

lava: melted rock that flows from a volcano

pollution: harmful materials that people release into the environment

sensor: a device used to sense and measure objects

tsunami: a huge ocean wave caused by an earthquake

Further Reading

Domaine, Helena. *Robotics.*
Minneapolis: Lerner Publications, 2006.

Hyland, Tony. *High-Risk Robots.* North Mankato,
MN: Smart Apple Media, 2008.

Idaho Public Television: Robot Facts
http://idahoptv.org/dialogue4kids/season10/robots
/facts.cfm

Parker, Steve. *Robots in Dangerous Places.*
Mankato, MN: Amicus, 2011.

Science Kids: Robots for Kids
http://www.sciencekids.co.nz/robots.html

Student Science—Cool Jobs: Wide World of Robots
https://student.societyforscience.org/article
/cool-jobs-wide-world-robots

Index

Photo Acknowledgments

The images in this book are used with the permission of: © Stephane Bidouze/
Shutterstock Images, pp. 2, 23; © Katsumi Kasahara/AP Images, pp. 4, 10, 15; © Keith
Srakocic/AP Images, p. 5; © Gary Tramontina/AP Images, p. 6; DARPA, p. 7;
© daseaford/Shutterstock Images, p. 8; © Yuriko Nakao/Reuters/Corbis, p. 9;
© Imagechina/AP Images, pp. 11, 30; © Issei Kato/Reuters/Corbis, p. 12; © Mike1024,
p. 13; John F. Williams/US Navy, p. 14; © Apichart Weerawong/AP Images, p. 16;
© Gerald Herbert/AP Images, p. 17; © Dave Tennenbaum/AP Images, p. 18; © Carnegie
Mellon University/AP Images, p. 19; USGS, p. 20; © Al Grillo/AP Images, p. 21;
© Goodluz/Shutterstock Images, pp. 22, 28; NASA, p. 24; © Steve Mitchell/AP Images,
p. 25; © Shizuo Kambayashi/AP Images, pp. 26, 31; US Navy, p. 27.

Front Cover: © DAVID BUIMOVITCH/AFP/Getty Images

Main body text set in Johann Light 30/36.